Zacchaeus

AMERICAN BIBLE SOCIETY
NEW YORK

Zacchaeus (Vol. 3)
Scripture quotes from the *Contemporary English Version*, Luke 19.1-10 (CEV). Wording and grammar represent the kind of language best understood and appreciated by young readers.

Copyright © 1995, American Bible Society
1865 Broadway, New York, N. Y. 10023
www.americanbible.org

Illustrations by Chantal Muller van den Berghe
Text by Bernard Hubler and Claude-Bernard Costecalde, Ph. D.
Design by Jacques Rey

Copyright © 1997, Éditions du Signe
Strasbourg, France
ISBN 1-58516-143-8
Printed in Italy
Eng. Port. CEV 560 P - 109860
ABS - 7/00 - 5,000

Sometimes we can hardly remember when we met someone for the first time.

At other times, the person we meet can make a very strong impression on us.

This is what happened to Zacchaeus when he met Jesus. Jesus touched Zacchaeus' heart and his life changed for the better.

Wouldn't you want to have your life changed in this way? Maybe you'll have an experience like this some day soon. Meeting Jesus today is still possible.
Jesus still speaks to us as he did to Zacchaeus:

Hurry down! I want to stay with you today!

Jesus was going through Jericho…

Jesus was on the street
in the town of Jericho.
The street was full of life.
Jesus loved life.
He went toward the crowd and the crowd came to meet him.

*To go toward others,
we must give of ourselves.*

... where a man named Zacchaeus lived.

Zacchaeus earned his living in Jericho as a tax collector. He was very dishonest and he tricked people out of their money. They disliked him and called him a cheat.

Some people try to cheat rather than to play fairly.

Zacchaeus wanted to see what Jesus was like... so he ran ahead.

Zacchaeus was curious about Jesus and wanted to see him, but he was a little man and couldn't see because of the crowd.
But Zacchaeus was clever. He always worked out how to get what he wanted. He ran ahead of Jesus.

There's always a way to get round obstacles.

He climbed up into a sycamore tree.

Zaccheus was comfortably
 perched in his tree.
 He felt sheltered,
 hidden among the leaves.
 Seeing things from above
he started thinking about his life.

Taking time to think things over can help us to see and to understand better.

When Jesus got there he looked up and said…

Jesus stopped at the foot of the tree
and saw Zacchaeus up in the branches.
This was a special moment for Zacchaeus.
Deep down, more than anything else,
he wanted to meet Jesus.
Jesus knew this and looked up at Zacchaeus
and spoke to him.

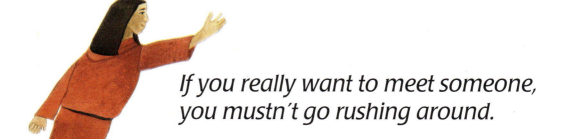

*If you really want to meet someone,
you mustn't go rushing around.*

"... Zacchaeus, hurry down! I want to stay with you today."

Jesus called Zacchaeus down and asked to stay with him. To welcome Jesus to his house, Zacchaeus had to climb down from the tree.
Of course, he also had to come down from the tree inside himself—the tree of his pride and of his lack of concern for others.

If you think that you are better than other people, or if you don't care about them, they'll never want to be with you.

Zacchaeus hurried down and gladly welcomed Jesus.

Zacchaeus got his house ready.
He was very honored to receive Jesus into his home.
He invited Jesus to stay for supper.
Zacchaeus was very happy.

*We don't invite just anybody to our home.
Friendship can develop by sharing a meal.*

Everyone who saw this started grumbling, "This man Zacchaeus is a sinner! And Jesus is going home to eat with him."

Jesus went to eat with someone whom everyone else thought was a sinner. People were shocked and they criticized Jesus severely.

Only people who do nothing are never criticized.

"I will give half of my property to the poor."

Because Jesus had spent time with him, Zacchaeus is no longer the same. He decides to make up for the bad things he had done. He discovered something that money can't buy: the happiness of being loved. From now on he will try to do good.

People who know they are loved are happier. Their life is changed.

"Today you and your family have been saved."

Jesus didn't arrive yesterday
and no one had to wait until tomorrow.
He is there today in Zacchaeus' house.
Today happiness arrives through Jesus.
Today everything has changed.
The same can be true for you today!

*Love can't wait for tomorrow.
We must show our love to others
today.*

26

As you were reading this book,
did it help you to see that the things Jesus did
and said are meant for you today?
When someone is with you in a special way you'll never be
exactly the same again.
Being together in this way changes something in our life.
Sometimes our whole life is completely changed.
But this won't happen if you behave like a turtle
and keep hiding in your shell.
You have to open your heart today
to welcome the One who invites himself into your home.

Jesus was going through Jericho…

… where a man named Zacchaeus lived.

Zacchaeus wanted to see what Jesus was like… so he ran ahead.

He climbed up into a sycamore tree.

When Jesus got there he looked up and said…

"… Zacchaeus, hurry down! I want to stay with you today."

Everyone who saw this started grumbling, "This man Zacchaeus is a sinner! And Jesus is going home to eat with him."

Zacchaeus hurried down and gladly welcomed Jesus.

"I will give half of my property to the poor."

"Today you and your family have been saved."

IN THE SAME COLLECTIONS:

The Good Samaritan
The Paralyzed Man
On the Road to Emmaus
Bartimaeus
The Call of the Disciples
The Calming of the Storm
Shared Bread
The Prodigal Son
An Amazing Catch
The Forgiven Sinner
The Farmer Who Went Out To Sow